Flexible Benefits

Philip Hutchinson

Acknowledgements

The CIPD would like to thank Philip Hutchinson of Jardine Lloyd Thompson Employee Benefits for managing and preparing this Executive Briefing, along with Helen Radcliffe and Neil Brennan for their contributions, Isabella Young for carrying out the research and Lisa Man for preparing and laying out this document. The following individuals who have been kind enough to comment on the material contained in this report are also to be thanked: Clive Wright, Steve Palmer, Stephen Turley and Linda Emmett.

The following organisations kindly contributed to the case studies used in this Executive Briefing: United Utilities; Nationwide Building Society; Financial Ombudsman; Cable & Wireless; Surrey County Council and The International Institute for Environment and Development.

The Chartered Institute of Personnel and Development is the leading publisher of books and reports for personnel and training professionals, students, and all those concerned with the effective management and development of people at work. For full details of all our titles, please contact the Publishing Department:

Tel: 020 8263 3387
Fax: 020 8263 3850

E-mail: publish@cipd.co.uk

To view and purchase the full range of CIPD publications:
www.cipd.co.uk/bookstore

Flexible Benefits

Philip Hutchinson
Head of Reward Consulting, Jardine Lloyd Thompson

© Chartered Institute of Personnel and Development 2004

All rights reserved. No part of this publication may be reproduced, stored in an information storage and retrieval system, or transmitted in any form or by any means, electronic, mechanical, photocopying, recording or otherwise without written permission of the Chartered Institute of Personnel and Development, CIPD House, Camp Road, London SW19 4UX.

First published 2004

Cover design by Curve
Designed and typeset by Beacon GDT
Printed in Great Britain by Short Run Press

British Library Cataloguing in Publication Data
A catalogue record for this book is available from the British Library

ISBN 1 84398 061 4

Chartered Institute of Personnel and Development,
CIPD House, Camp Road, London SW19 4UX

Tel: 020 8971 9000
Fax: 020 8263 3333
Website: www.cipd.co.uk

Incorporated by Royal Charter. Registered charity no. 1079797.

Contents

Foreword		vii
Executive summary		ix
Chapter 1	What are flexible benefits?	1
Chapter 2	Building a business case for flexible benefits	7
Chapter 3	Strategy and design	15
Chapter 4	Pensions and flexible benefits	23
Chapter 5	Tax and employment law issues	29
Chapter 6	Documentation, scheme launch and communications	33
Chapter 7	Management and administration	39
Chapter 8	Installation, implementation and outsourcing	47
Chapter 9	Where next for flex?	53
Chapter 10	Are you ready for flex?	59
References and bibliography		65

Foreword

Flexible benefits are not new. As a concept, flexible benefits schemes (also known as 'cafeteria benefits' or 'flex plan') have been around for about two decades. What is new, however, is that more employers seem to be using them. Research by the CIPD and others shows an increase in the proportion of employers offering such schemes and a large number of organisations actively investigating the possibility of introducing a flex plan in the workplace.

While there may be many benefits from adopting a flex plan, such as aligning the reward and business strategies with one another or managing the cost of future benefits provision, employers need to consider whether such a scheme is right for them.

To help organisations evaluate whether a flexible benefits scheme makes sense for them, the CIPD has produced this Executive Briefing. It does not concentrate on what a flexible benefits scheme is, or why employers have been introducing them. Various publications and articles have already covered both these issues extensively (see the References section). Nor is this a 'how-to' guide for people to have on their desk as they implement a flexible benefits scheme. Instead, this Briefing aims to give a strategic overview of the key issues that employers should consider before introducing such an initiative at their workplace.

As well as covering some of the crucial design issues, it also examines some of the important implementation issues. This is because research, including that carried out by the CIPD, finds that reward initiatives tend to fail, not because employers do not address the design issue, but because they overlook the importance of implementation. They concentrate on the 'what' rather than the 'how'.

To try and redress this imbalance, this Briefing indicates some of the implementation issues that employers should consider at the outset, such as, 'How will flex fit in with the reward, HR and business strategies?' Those employers who consider how a flexible benefits scheme will support their business goals and assist the aims and objectives of the HR and reward strategies will find it easier to successfully implement such a scheme and see more positive results. Also, by setting objectives, organisations will find it easier to judge whether the initiative is a success or not. At the start, organisations need to consider what measures of success they should adopt to evaluate and monitor the scheme.

Similarly, employers need to consider: How will the scheme be implemented? How will the project be managed? How will a feasibility study be carried out? How will the scheme be administered? And how will it be communicated?

This last point needs special consideration; initiatives, including reward, can founder on an organisation's inability to communicate effectively to its staff. For flex plans to work, employees need to know *what* they are being given and *why*, *how* it will work and *when* it will be introduced. The organisation should also try and engage them in its development, so that employees feel a sense of ownership in the initiative; they need an almost constant supply of information to explain how the scheme will, and does, work.

As well as these issues, this Briefing also raises technical implementation questions for employers to consider. For instance, how will the new flex scheme relate to the existing occupational pension plans? How will it interact with legal and taxation issues? How will the various stakeholders, such as HR, pensions, payroll and finance, work with one another?

However, as some HR commentators point out, just as important as the 'how' is the 'who'. Employers should consider who are the most able people to carry out a feasibility study to see if flex is the right option for the organisation. If flex is the answer, which key people should be in the implementation team to look at scheme strategy and design? And who are the best communicators in the organisation to sell the initiative to staff?

This Briefing does not attempt to answer all these questions. The solutions for each organisation will differ, depending upon their own set of individual circumstances, but it highlights their existence and employers need to be prepared to tackle them. Flexible benefits can bring tangible benefits to an organisation as part of an integrated and aligned total rewards strategy, but only if employers address the implementation issues as well as the design issues.

Charles Cotton
CIPD Adviser, Reward

If after reading this book you have any questions, please feel free to contact either the author, Philip Hutchinson on philip_hutchinson@jtlgroup.com, or myself at c.cotton@cipd.co.uk.

Executive summary

- A flexible benefits scheme (also known as 'cafeteria benefits' or 'flex plan') is any arrangement that gives employees a choice over the mix of cash and benefits they receive.

- For the employer, the benefits of operating a flex scheme include adapting to a changing labour market, better targeting of benefits, and creating and enforcing an employer brand. It can also improve the way that the value of the reward package is communicated to staff in order to give them a better understanding and appreciation of the benefit spend.

- For employees, the benefits can include wider choice. It also allows them to tailor their total reward package towards changes in lifestyle, such as marriage or promotion.

- In the past, complexity and cost of administration have been the major barriers to introducing flexible benefits. These days new technology, better ways of working and the availability of specialist third-party administration have reduced these barriers.

- Flexible benefits may not always be the right solution and therefore an extensive feasibility study should be undertaken to confirm the right choice.

- The study should build a substantial business case for its introduction, ensure the culture is ready for such a concept and determine how best to communicate the new scheme.

- The feasibility study should put a price on the costs and benefits of the initiative. For instance, if trying to improve business performance, the study should examine how much such costs as recruitment, selection, turnover and training will need to fall over time before a flexible benefits scheme becomes a worthwhile investment, and whether these falls are realistic.

- Designing a flexible benefits plan does not have to be a long complex process. It can be simplified to answering a series of related questions, most of which need some research/data collection or advice to enable the employer to reach the answer.

- The practicality of designing a flexible benefits scheme includes: determining when the scheme will be introduced; how it will be administered; what benefits will be provided; and how it will be communicated.

Flexible Benefits
Executive Summary

- The administration, IT and internal structure must be able to support the new design and employer needs. It needs to ensure that whatever strategy is developed, it can be communicated effectively.

- Historically, pensions have been viewed as one of the most difficult benefits to include in a flexible benefit plan. This position has changed somewhat in recent years, due to the general move in the pensions market from defined benefits to defined contribution schemes, as the latter are much easier to incorporate into a flex plan.

- There are still some arguments against incorporating pension schemes into flex plans. The employer needs to weigh this up against the advantages of doing so at an early stage in the scheme design process.

- It is important that any organisation introducing a flexible benefits scheme understands the impact on the scheme of taxation treatment and the possible consequence of not dealing with any employment law issues that may arise.

- Education is a vital component of communicating a flexible benefits scheme. Employees should understand the options available to them and the consequences of their decisions, because they will ultimately be responsible for them.

- A good communication strategy should set out to determine what needs communicating, who to communicate to, what media should be used, who will do the communicating and the best timing.

- The management of a flexible benefits scheme involves co-ordination of several different elements. These include the administration team, HR function, payroll function, product providers, helpdesk function and IT function.

- It is advisable to install the system as soon as possible to ensure time for communicating and testing, and that service standards set are realistic.

- With the growing popularity of flexible benefits plans, there is a growing desire among organisations that have operated flex for a number of years to develop their schemes to make them more appealing to employees and to ensure they do more for the sponsoring employer. However, you can only go so far adding new benefits to the menu on offer and there are only so many choices an employee can make.

- As the expertise in flexible benefits schemes builds up (particularly with third-party administrators), those involved in this field are looking at more exciting ways of using flexible benefits plans. These include: opening up enrolment to more than once a year;

development of worksite marketing; and industry-wide (rather than unique-to-individual-organisation) flexible benefits plans. Also on the horizon are profit-related and extended flexible benefits schemes.

This chapter covers:

- what flexible benefits are
- how flexible benefits work and
- how they can deliver business benefits to organisations.

1 | What are flexible benefits?

Introduction

A flexible benefits scheme (also known as 'cafeteria benefits' or 'flex plan') is any arrangement that gives employees a choice over the mix of cash and benefits they receive. At its simplest, it might be the choice between a car and additional cash. More sophisticated programmes give employees choices between different benefits, or offer a range of options within one benefit category such as the choices of self or family medical insurance. Flexible benefits should not be confused with voluntary benefits, where employers offer staff the opportunity to purchase third-party products or services at a discounted rate.

For the employer, some of the benefits of operating a flex plan can include:

- helping align the total rewards strategy to the HR and business strategies

- making sure rewards match the needs of an increasingly diverse, demanding and ageing workforce

- ensuring value for money through better targeting of benefits by enabling the organisation to make employee rewards more attractive without increasing costs

- allowing employers to cap the cost of benefits in the future

- creating and enforcing a recognisable employer brand, although, if more employers adopt flex in the future, offering this type of scheme on its own will no longer be enough to stand out from the crowd. If this becomes the case, organisations will need to consider differentiating the 'how' rather than the 'what'

- enhancing perceived value of the benefits package, as staff are able to choose the mix of cash and benefits that best meets their needs

- underpinning and facilitating cultural change

- harmonising and rationalising different sets of benefits

- helping react to changes in legislation, such as government proposals on pensions and retirement.

From an employee's perspective the advantages can include:

- improve choice

- take advantage of employer's 'bulk buying' power to afford products and pricing at preferential levels

- tailor benefit package to lifestyle and changes in lifestyle

- give a sense of control and involvement

- help manage balance between changing world of work, lifestyle, work style and personal finances.

In this Briefing we will be referring to a selection of companies that kindly agreed to provide case studies. This will be through a mix of quotations and charts. The research shows that there is no such thing as a standard flexible benefits scheme. Each is dependent on the organisation and its unique situation.

The growth of flex

In the past, flexible benefits schemes have usually been more talked about than implemented. Research used to show that many employers said they were actively considering introducing a flexible benefits scheme, yet when subsequent enquiries were carried out, few had actually managed to implement a scheme, being put off by the cost and administration.

Yet research appears to indicate that this may be changing. The CIPD revealed that in 2001, around 9 per cent of employers had a flex plan; by 2002, this had increased to 12 per cent, with a further two-fifths considering its introduction. *Employee*

Table 1 | Background to companies used for case studies in this Briefing

Company	Sector	No. employees in scheme	No. years scheme running
A	private	4,500	1
B	private	15,000	5
C	private	620	3
D	private	5,000	7
E	public	23,500	7
F	charity	64	2

Benefits magazine showed a rise from 9 per cent in 2002 to 19 per cent in 2003 in the proportion of employers offering this type of benefit.

The latest study from Incomes Data Services points to a rise in the number of employers 'becoming convinced of the case for flexible benefits as concerns over the practical barriers to implementation lessen'.

Another reason why employers are considering flex is that employment and lifestyles are changing. Many organisations no longer consider that a traditional reward structure of a basic salary and fixed benefits is the best way to meet the needs of an increasingly diverse and demanding workforce.

How flex can save costs

A flexible benefits scheme can also lead to savings. By targeting benefits to where they are needed by employees, it is possible to save the cost of providing unwanted benefits. National Insurance, income tax and VAT savings can be achieved through more efficient payment structures. Further savings can be made through the additional buying power available to employers and their employee benefit advisers.

A well-designed flexible benefits programme that is part of an integrated total reward strategy can reduce costs in other ways. For instance, it may help reduce staff turnover or help attract more job applicants, thereby reducing the costs spent on recruitment, selection and training newly recruited employees.

It can also be used to manage future costs, especially long-term social and welfare benefits, such as PMI or critical health insurance.

How flex can facilitate change

The introduction of flexible benefits can facilitate a variety of organisational changes. These include:

- moving to a defined contribution (money purchase) pension scheme

- restructuring company car schemes

- integrating incompatible terms and conditions after mergers and acquisitions

- introducing new payment systems

- reinforcing cultural changes.

> '*By targeting benefits to where they are needed by employees, it is possible to save the cost of providing unwanted benefits.*'

How flexible benefits schemes work

Each employee is provided with the cash value of his or her existing rewards, together with a menu of benefits and cash. Employees then choose the combination of cash and benefits that best suits them.

Employees can alter their choices at fixed regular intervals, subject to any longer term commitments, such as cars and some insured benefits. It is also possible to allow non-regular adjustments to take account of lifestyle changes, such as setting up a home, parenthood, etc. Many employers insist that employees retain certain core benefits that are essential for their welfare, such as a minimum level of holiday, accident insurance and life cover. Employers may also install a system that maintains the perception of pay and reward grades. Creating a mix of core cash, flexible benefits and core benefits does this.

Employees can also vary the extent of a chosen benefit. For example, with medical insurance, an employee could have a choice of family medical cover, partner cover or single cover.

How flex can bring added value

Flexible benefits have many benefits for the employer – better targeting of employer costs to save unnecessary overprovision, a workforce in which all individuals feel that they are being looked after, and a modern image in the recruitment market and elsewhere.

However, there are further added values. For instance, it can be used to communicate the true cost of pay and benefits. A cash price is placed on existing benefits; employees can then exchange these benefits for cash, and conversely cash can be exchanged for benefits.

Businesses can be protected from the risks of the rising cost of benefits. Within a flexible benefits scheme each employee takes responsibility for choosing his or her own mix of benefits, taking into account any cost increases.

It is easier for a business to make continuous improvements to its pay and benefits structures. If new and attractive benefits come on to the market, these can be offered to employees; conversely, if benefits become more costly, this is reflected in the pricing. However, to achieve business goals it is important that flexible benefits are part of an integrated total reward strategy.

Basic flexible benefits process

There is no such thing as a standard flexible benefits process. Each is dependent on the organisation and its unique situation. However, most follow a similar process to the four-step process outlined below, namely:

1. The employer designs and presents a menu of benefits, including prices. These can be illustrated in an employee handbook, which also contains the rules and regulations governing the scheme, the options available, and a short description of each of the products in the menu and the tax effect on them. Also included in the handbook will be an explanation of if and how employees can use some of their salary, bonuses or holidays to trade for flexible benefits.

   Prices are usually included in a preference form, which is used by the individual to calculate and select the mix of benefits that they want.

The preference form is usually in an electronic or paper form, which is relatively easier and cheaper to change than the employee handbook.

Traditional schemes allow employees to make their selection once a year. There are, however, an increasing number of plans that allow quarterly changes and have an additional range of products that can be selected at any time. There are special circumstances – mainly changes in lifestyle – where employees may be able to make their change outside of these fixed dates.

2. Employees select their preferred combination of cash and benefits to match their needs. This should be double-checked by the administrative department to ensure that no limits have been exceeded and the correct information has been supplied.

3. The employer approves the employee's preferences and the information is processed. This approval may also extend to the line manager's approval for buying and selling holidays to ensure proper management of respective teams.

4. The employer notifies all the providers and suitable arrangements are made for transfer of money to them from employer and employee, following selection. A benefits statement is also issued to employees as a record of what they have chosen.

This chapter looks at:

- how to conduct a research and employee benefits review

- the issues to consider when planning how to communicate the scheme

- the importance of examining whether the investment in the scheme is worthwhile

- possible performance measures to consider when monitoring and evaluating the impact of the scheme in the future.

2 | Building a business case for flexible benefits

Introduction

An increasing pace of change in the business environment, including mergers and acquisitions, fuelled by more realistic costings and improved administration is leading to an increased interest in flexible benefits among employers.

However, flexible benefits may not always be the right solution and an extensive feasibility study should be undertaken to ensure that its introduction is the right choice for the organisation. The main objective is to build a substantial business case for its introduction, ensure the culture is ready for such a concept and determine the best way of communicating the new scheme.

Q: What process did you have to go through to get the approval to go ahead and introduce a flexible benefits scheme?

A: The flexible benefits package was part of a larger employee self-service scheme allowing employees to do many transactions online, such as expenses, overtime or holidays. This was part of a strategy to change the overall culture of the company and to maximise electronic communication, as all 4,500 staff now have online access to the scheme.
Company A

> *'The success of the study will depend on the quality of information and statistics gathered at the commencement of the project. There are a variety of tools and techniques that can be used.'*

Research

The success of the study will depend on the quality of information and statistics gathered at the commencement of the project. There are a variety of tools and techniques that can be used. The main areas of research include:

- internal fact-find
- competitive benchmarking
- benefit audits
- employee preferences surveys and focus groups
- administration process and IT infrastructure assessment
- communications audit
- evaluation against good practice.

From this research there are 11 key areas that need to be assessed, to determine if flexible benefits are the best solution for the organisation and, if so, ensure a complete and robust business case for its introduction. These are outlined below:

1. Supporting and enhancing the organisation's mission statement and key priorities

The success of any policy and/or strategy is based on the defining principles that they are built on. Because of the holistic and interactive influence that flexible benefits will have on all parts of the organisation, these principles are both pivotal and important. Some of the key principles that need to be established include:

- How will the new scheme support and enhance the total reward strategy, the HR strategy and the business strategy?

- What are the aims and objectives of the new flexible benefits scheme?

- What are the guiding principles for the new flexible benefits scheme?

Q: What did you expect to get from having a flexible benefits scheme?

A: A package that enabled employees to make a choice of benefits that met their individual needs. In our situation of a merger, it meant that individuals could stick with the benefits they had previously and take advantage of new ones.
Company C

2. Employee benefits review

The next stage in the process should be to carry out an audit of the existing benefits packages. The benefits review should attempt to respond to some of the following key issues:

- what benefits are provided and for whom

- take-up rates where benefits are optional

- who the benefit providers are

- what the contracts/costs with the providers are

- what the contractual obligations to employees are

- how the benefits will be managed/administered

- whether to limit the degree of flex on certain benefits

- is the aim to cut or cap benefit costs or enhance the employer brand?

This will allow the review to be put in proper context by establishing what the current arrangements are and what limits there are on what is achievable, and will provide information that can be used to assess the impact of any proposed changes.

3. Market issues

Whatever the driver is in considering a flexible benefits scheme, there must be clearly defined market reasons (either labour market or the business market) for introducing it. Even in the case of harmonisation of staff terms and conditions, where there is no immediate link, without such consideration the new scheme could work against the organisation's interests in the marketplace, if it is not planned correctly. Examples of market-driven issues include:

- faster pace of business and organisational change

- higher employer and employee expectations, staff productivity and HR returns as the company grows

- increasingly diverse and ageing UK workforce

- tightening UK labour market

- retention, motivation and recruitment of staff.

4. HR issues

The most important part of examining the HR issues for introducing a new scheme is to establish the main reason for considering the scheme from both the employer's and employee's perspective. For example, the employer may see a flexible benefits scheme as a way of harmonising two sets of staff benefits, while employees may favour a flex scheme because it allows them to choose the benefits that are most attractive to them. Some of the key HR issues that an organisation needs to establish include:

- a clear picture of employee preferences

- the logistics and ramifications of the consolidation/harmonisation of reward structures

- the effect on perceived value of total reward packages

- the effect on long-term costs of employee benefits.

5. Employment law issues

As the complexity and amount of new legislation continue to rise in the UK, it is important to consider employment law aspects. Key employment issues to consider include:

- the consequences of any direct or indirect change to the terms and conditions of employment

- the effect of current and proposed legislation

- the TUPE effect where relevant

- the possibility that the new scheme structure will unintentionally create discrimination.

6. Communications issues

Effective communication is more an art form than a science. Organisational culture is made up of individuals, so there can never be a 'one-size-fits-all' solution. The study should set out to develop a framework and define alternative steps to implement an effective communication strategy. Some of the key issues a communication strategy should address include:

- branding, style and timing

- what needs communicating

- who are you going to communicate to

- what media will be used

- who will be the communicators.

7. Product selection and mix

At this stage of the project, the study needs to recommend the policy and strategy for the scheme and the basic structure of the products and how they are mixed together. The organisation also needs to decide the costing structure for the products, whether the organisation or the individual will pay (ie employer-sponsored products or voluntary benefits paid for by employees, though there could be a mix, for instance with PMI where an employer pays for single cover as a core and an employee can trade up at their expense), as well as the rules and regulations that will bind them all together. Factors that need to be considered when selecting the policy and portfolio include:

- policy and strategy for scheme based on employee and employer preferences

- consequences and costs of restructuring existing products, eg PMI

- consequences of introducing new products, eg voluntary benefits

- contractual situation regarding existing benefits

- risk analysis of staff making poor choices, eg pensions or health cover.

Employee preferences (please refer to Chapter 6 for details of how these can be ascertained) and corporate requirements will drive the choice of products for the scheme. To begin with, the initial selection of products will probably be too many to effectively administer, and a process of elimination will be required to develop a more manageable portfolio. This is best done by considering the priority each individual product has, compared to its ease of administration and cost.

8. Administration, IT and outsourcing

As well as establishing affordability and ease of managing, the study should ensure that the systems and processes provide security, service and good value.

Some of the key administration, IT and outsourcing issues that should be considered include:

- ability of current infrastructure and IT system to cope with proposed scheme

- feasibility of using new technology such as web-based IT

- whether to administer scheme in-house or outsource, including resources required

- how to deal with staff who have not made their benefit selections within the set time period

- integration with HR and payroll systems

- management and monitoring of new scheme.

If the decision is to use the organisation's in-house systems, there will be a need to assess the infrastructure required to process the various transactions created.

However, if the organisation is considering outsourcing, it will need to be aware that while it may be beneficial, this is a complex process that needs careful management. Time is needed to select the service provider and to identify any potential difficulties.

9. Project management

Flexible benefits are, by their very nature, complex and holistic. Management of such projects requires a special approach based on key tasks and timescales.

The feasibility study should establish from the outset how much of this project management will be carried out within the organisation and what, if any, will be the demands on external providers and consultants.

10. Financial benefits, costs and risk analysis

A crucial part of the process is to work out whether the benefits and advantages of the proposed flexible benefits scheme are worth the cost of investment and the risk.

Costs are relatively easy to work out. However, benefits can be harder to ascertain at the outset. If the aim is to cap, or even cut, benefit costs, such an analysis will be relatively easy to carry out. If the objective is to become an 'employer of choice' it will be harder to predict what the impact of the flex plan over time will be on such performance measures as recruitment, selection, turnover and training costs – especially if the flex initiative is part of an integrated and aligned approach towards reward and recognition.

However, in these instances, the project team can calculate what the recruitment, selection, turnover and training costs are for the organisation, and gauge how much these will need to fall to make the introduction of flexible benefits worthwhile – and whether such falls are achievable.

11. Monitoring and evaluation

The final part of the study is to think about how the organisation can assess the impact of the flexible benefits scheme. Obviously, a flexible benefits scheme will interact with other ways an organisation rewards and recognises its staff; therefore, it will be hard in practice to attribute, say a fall in staff turnover, solely to the flexible benefits scheme. However, in the round, if you have introduced a flexible benefits scheme to enhance your employer brand, then you would expect it to have a positive impact on turnover. Therefore, it is important that you collect and analyse the data to assess that this is actually the case. Possible HR measures an organisation can use to assess the impact of the flex plan over time can include the following:

- staff take-up rate
- staff turnover rates and costs
- absence rates and costs
- training costs
- recruitment and selection costs
- number of applications per job vacancy and ratio of acceptances
- cost of the overall benefit package
- staff commitment and/or satisfaction.

Possible business measures can include:

- earnings per share
- market share

Table 2 | Case studies: Investment in time and money (£,000s)

Company	Budgeted cost	Actual cost	Budgeted time	Actual time
A	Not available	Not available	90 days	90 days
B	100	100	1 year	2 years
C	Not available	Not available	4 months	4 months
D	250	350	9 to 12 months	1 year
E	Not available	Not available	1 year	1 year
F	20	20	1 year	2 years

- customer/client/voter satisfaction

- waste

- profit

- sales growth.

The final report

The final report should be based on policies and strategies, rather than detail. For instance, it should examine the types of products that should be included in the scheme and their basic cost and administration requirements, as opposed to the full details of specification and individual/corporate costs.

The amount of money and resources allocated to the study usually determines how detailed it is. However, this is an important part of the project and it usually forms the foundation stone for the new scheme.

There are many reasons why an employer may be considering a flex plan scheme (such as a vehicle for delivering a unique offering to staff); however, if the business case for flex plan is not proven, an employer may wish to explore other options to meet its objectives, for instance, a voluntary benefits scheme, or total reward and benefit statements.

This chapter covers:

- setting scheme objectives, messages and success criteria

- carrying out a review of both benefits and benefit providers

- carrying out a funding review.

3 | Strategy and design

Introduction

Designing a flexible benefits plan does not have to be a long-drawn-out and complex process. It can be simplified down to answering a whole series of related questions, most of which need some research/data collection or advice to help you reach an answer. Once answers to all these questions have been found, then you will have the necessary information to put together a series of rules that will govern the way the scheme will work.

The key questions that need to be answered are set out in the sections below.

Practicalities

Before you get down to the nitty-gritty of the scheme design, you need to answer some fundamental questions that will have an impact on the design of your scheme. These are:

- **When are you looking to introduce the scheme?**

The less time you have available, the simpler the scheme needs to be. You can always develop complexity later.

- **How will you be administering the scheme?**

If you are using a paper-based system and/or a spreadsheet to manage the scheme, you need to ensure the scheme is simple enough for this to be achievable. If you are using a web-enabled system, you can afford to include more benefits and have a more complex scheme design.

- **Project management**

It is advisable that a joint project team is formed to manage, co-ordinate and drive through the various key tasks required. The best way forward is a partnership approach to project management, which balances specialist management skills and advice with local knowledge and resources.

- **Selecting external advisers**

If the decision has been taken to use external advisers to manage all or some of the design and administration of the scheme, then an agreement needs to be drawn up defining their contribution and input to it, along with anticipated timescales and costings.

Benefits

You can then move on to more specific questions relating to the benefits that will be provided under the scheme. These are:

- **What benefits do you currently provide (and at what levels) and who do you provide them for?**

The starting point for the design of your scheme will be your current benefit provisions, because for legal reasons, you will want employees to be able to change their current benefit packages once a flex scheme has been introduced.

- **What benefits must you provide in the future?**

The employment contracts you give your employees will have some references to benefits in them and it is important to know what you must provide, going forward, so that this can be built into the scheme design.

> *'Benefits should not all be introduced straight away as a flex plan should be an evolving animal with new benefits being introduced each year to maintain interest.'*

- **What benefits do you want employees to have in the future and at what minimum levels?**

The organisation will need to consider what type of employer it wants to be. Does it want to give employees total freedom to choose what they want, with the risk that some staff may not select wisely? Or does it feel a 'moral' obligation to provide some specific benefits it does not want employees to opt out of totally, for example life insurance? However, it may be that you would be happy for them to reduce the level of cover they have, eg from four times salary to two times salary. Once you have identified these benefits and the minimum levels of cover, these will form the core elements of the flex plan.

- **What benefits do your employees want?**

It is a useful exercise to find out what your employees would like to see as part of their benefits package so that you design a scheme that is going to be attractive to them. Possible ways of gauging this include staff surveys, surveys of former employees or special focus groups – though such research has to be handled with care, as there is the danger of raising expectations that cannot be met.

Benefits should not all be introduced straight away as a flex plan should be an evolving animal with new benefits being introduced each year to maintain interest; therefore, you should prioritise these desired benefits to ensure that you introduce the most popular first.

Employers also need to consider which employees they are going to offer the flex plan to. To all or to a particular group of staff? If for all, you need to consider if it makes sense to phase it in by workgroup or site, or introduce it across the organisation in one go.

- **What benefits is it feasible to provide?**

You and your employees may have very definite ideas about what benefits should be in the scheme. However, there may well be some things that restrict what you can actually do in practice. For example, you may have a defined benefit pension scheme that would be complex to integrate into a flex plan, or the administration system you will be using cannot cope easily with a particular benefit or form of benefit. Also, the cost of provision may change if providers know that the benefit is now optional and you lose the power of bulk purchase.

- **Who do you want to be able to select for each of the benefits?**

There may be some benefits that you currently provide, or which you are looking to introduce, that are not suitable for all your employees, eg company cars or car allowances. These should be identified and your scheme set up in such a way that employees can only select from a restricted range of benefits. For ease of administration, and for the overall impression given by the scheme, it can be better to let as many employees as possible have access to each benefit. This also allows you to get the best financial terms possible for the benefits you want to offer. However, this has to be weighed up against the overall cost of providing those benefits

To counteract the possible impact on employees of seeing all the benefits that managers are entitled to, but which they are not, employers should also consider different material for different employee groups.

Once you have answered these questions you will be able to determine:

- what benefits you will initially provide under the scheme
- what options within each benefit you will offer
- who will be able to select which options
- what benefits will be core
- what benefits you will look to introduce in future years.

Typical flexible benefit products

Table 3 indicates the range of possible products that can be offered under a flexible benefit scheme.

Funding

An important element of the scheme design will be its financial elements. The answers to the following questions will define how the financial aspects of the scheme will work in future.

- **How much money will you give your employees to spend on their benefits?**

A common approach is to establish a benefit allowance, which employees can then use to buy the benefits they wish. This is normally set at a level that will allow employees to replicate the benefits package they had pre-flex. This can be set to include the costs of the core benefits (to get over the total value of the benefits package), which are then deducted against the core benefits. You also need to consider whether or not you want to add any further company contribution to the benefit allowance.

Going forward, a typical approach is to maintain the benefit allowance at the level required to keep the pre-flex benefits package. However, one of the principles of flex is that it breaks the link between the cost of the benefits and the amount the employer gives employees to spend on their benefits. This is because employees, as a condition of participating in the flex plan, sign up to the concept that the menu of benefits, the prices of the benefits and the benefit allowance can all change from year to year. There is no guarantee they will be able to keep the same package at all points in the future. Therefore, you are free to set the allowance at whatever level you wish.

- **How much of their own cash will employees be allowed to spend on their benefits?**

In many cases schemes are set up so that employees can spend their full benefit allowance on benefits, or they can choose to spend less and take the remainder as additional cash, or spend more and have their base pay reduced accordingly. However, if you wish, you can set schemes up so that only the benefit allowance is available to spend on benefits and no salary sacrifice can be made. You can also set limits on how much of an employee's cash they can spend on benefits to ensure your employees retain enough money to

Table 3 | Case studies: products for flexible benefits schemes

Original benefits offered				
Partner life insurance	PMI	Partner health screen	Medical cash plan	PC leasing
Childcare vouchers	Trading holidays	Health club	Dental care	Roadside assistance
Defined benefit and defined contribution pension	Accidental accident insurance	Critical illness insurance	Travel insurance	AVCs
Benefits added since scheme started				
Pension top-up	Retail shopping vouchers	Positive care cancer plan	Paperless childcare vouchers	Defined contribution pension
Possible products for the future				
Bicycles	Flexible pensions	Clothing vouchers	Cars	Gym membership
Chiropody	Optical care	Alternative healthcare		

live on and the cash/benefit relationships are not distorted.

The answers to these questions will set the financial constraints on the scheme.

Providers

The final key element of the scheme design will be to select your benefit providers. The answers to the following questions will help you to finalise this.

- **Who provides your existing benefits and can/will they provide benefits on a flexible basis?**

Your existing benefit providers may not be willing or able to accommodate the provision of benefits on a flexible basis. If this is the case, you will need to seek alternative suppliers. Even if they can provide the benefits for your flex plan, they may not be able to offer the best prices or terms and conditions. Many benefit providers, especially for insured benefits, will significantly increase their premiums where you allow your employees to opt out of benefits because they are no longer able to pool risk. Others will also severely restrict the way in which choices can be made, for example making employees keep the same choice for longer than a year, or not allowing employees to jump between extreme levels of cover. You need to understand early on what your existing benefit providers can and cannot do.

Are there other suppliers who could provide benefits on a flexible basis at a good price, for both existing and new benefits?

There will be other suppliers out in the marketplace that will be able to provide the benefits on the basis you are looking for. It is generally a good idea to carry out a market review for each benefit when introducing a flex plan to ensure you get the best possible prices, the best levels of cover and the most attractive administration arrangements.

The answers to these questions will give you the final details for the main parts of the scheme design.

General rules

There are various other elements to the scheme design covering issues such as when changes to benefits can be made, what happens if an employee goes on maternity leave, etc. Most schemes will allow changes only once a year, but will also permit amendments for major events such as births, marriage and divorce – usually called 'lifestyle events'. The answers to these questions need to be incorporated into the final rules of the scheme, which then need to be approved by the Inland Revenue.

The major rules should cover the following:

- When will new joiners be able to make benefit selections?

- When will the annual enrolment period be?

- What events will be classified as lifestyle events?

- What benefits can be changed on a lifestyle event?

- What will the financial value of a flexible option be based on?

- How much of their salary can employees use to trade for flexible benefits?

- Will there be an option for employees to 'cash in' unused benefits at the end of the scheme year?

- Will employees have to sign their Preference Form before confirmation of choice is given?

- Will all flexible benefits cease immediately an employee leaves the company?

- Will there be a refund for unused benefits, once selected and approved?

This chapter covers:

- should existing occupational pension arrangements be included in a flexible benefits scheme?

- options for including a defined benefits pension scheme within a flex plan

- options for including a defined contributions pension scheme within a flex plan

- other issues around incorporating an occupational pension scheme within flex, including: communication, contractual obligations, pension scheme rules and salary sacrifice.

4 | Pensions and flexible benefits

Introduction

Historically, pensions have been viewed as one of the most difficult benefits to include in a flexible benefits plan. This was mainly because many company schemes were defined benefit plans and the practical issues surrounding incorporating these into flex plans were felt to be too much of a hurdle, especially when an organisation was having to deal with the general complexities of introducing flex.

The position has changed somewhat in recent years, owing to the general move in the pensions market from defined benefit to defined contribution schemes, as the latter are much easier to incorporate into a flex plan. The advancement of flexible benefit management and communication systems, using the web, has also made the incorporation of pension schemes into flex much easier.

Should pensions be included or not?

There are still some arguments against incorporating pension schemes into flex plans and these need to be very carefully weighed up against the advantages of doing so at an early stage in the scheme design process.

The table below summarises some pros and cons of incorporating pensions into flex.

Table 4 | The pros and cons of incorporating pensions into flex

Pros	Cons
should raise awareness of the organisation's pension provisions	can still be complex to set up and manage
can help to increase membership of the pension scheme	providing flexibility could encourage employees to opt out of the scheme
can help 'sweeten the pill' of moving from defined benefit to defined contribution pension provision	could increase membership of the scheme, which could lead to increased pension costs
potential cost savings from utilising salary sacrifice arrangements	allowing employees more choice over their pension arrangements could lead to more questions and the need for education to be given to employees

Options for including pensions

Obviously the options available for incorporating your pension arrangements into a flexible benefits plan will very much depend on what pension arrangements you have in place and your future plans for pension provision.

Additional voluntary contributions

If you operate an occupational pension scheme, it is commonplace to offer scheme members an additional voluntary contribution (AVC) scheme to allow them to top up their pension provision. In most cases this will be a money purchase facility. As a minimum, you should consider incorporating this into the flex plan. This would simply be a way of raising the profile of the AVC scheme and encourage employees to contribute to it.

Defined benefit / final salary schemes

If you currently provide a final salary scheme for your employees, and are going to be maintaining it, then there are a number of options available for incorporating this into a flex plan:

- If it is felt that it is too complex to provide flexibility within a final salary scheme you can simply provide a money purchase top-up facility, either using an AVC facility or a separate money purchase top-up section.

- You could simply retain the existing accrual rate, but vary the 'employee' contribution each year to share some of the risks and costs associated with such arrangements.

- You could offer different levels of pension accrual, eg 50ths, 60ths, 70ths and 80ths, each with different levels of employee contribution.

With such arrangements there are many things to consider before deciding on the best approach for your organisation, namely:

- How frequently will you allow employees to change their selections? It may not be practical to have them opting for 50ths one year and 80ths the next. It may be more sensible to make them stick to their selections for a number of years.

- Will your pension scheme administrators be able to effectively manage such an arrangement (eg keep the appropriate records, get the calculations right)?

- How will the actuary to your scheme react to such an arrangement and how will it affect the funding of the scheme?

- Will the introduction of flexibility mean the investment strategy of the scheme has to change?

Incorporating a defined benefit scheme into a flex plan is a complex process and can have significant implications. Therefore it should only be attempted with the right advice and assistance.

**Defined contribution /
money purchase schemes**

These types of arrangements can take several different forms and legal bases – occupational money purchase schemes, group personal pension plans and stakeholder schemes. However, they are all very similar in how they work and are easy to incorporate into flex plans.

With all these arrangements there are two key elements that employees generally have flexibility over, namely, the level of contributions they want to make and the funds they want their contributions to be invested in.

When incorporating such pension plans into a flexible benefits scheme, from a risk perspective it is better to separate these two elements, with employees selecting their contribution levels within the flex plan and investment selections being dealt with elsewhere (generally directly with the pension provider or the investment manager).

Enrolment forms for the flex plan can be designed (whether they are electronic or paper-based) to incorporate most contribution structures, such as:

- age-related employer contributions

- minimum employee contributions required before employer contributions are made

- waiting periods before employer contributions can be made

- employer/employee matching contribution scales.

One important issue that must be considered is how often employees will be allowed to change their pension contributions. In a flex plan, other than for lifestyle changes, employees are generally restricted to making benefit selections once a year. With many pension schemes, especially stakeholder arrangements, employees have much more flexibility and are allowed to change their contribution levels whenever they like and can also decide to pay fixed amounts into the scheme or percentages of their salary. The extent to which this should be mirrored in the flex plan needs to be carefully considered, and any restrictions on what can and cannot be imposed by the flex administration system need to be identified.

On the whole, apart from the considerations identified above, incorporating a defined contribution pension plan into a flex scheme is a relatively easy process.

> *'Raising the profile of pensions through flex will often make employees think about their pension provision more frequently.'*

Other issues

Other considerations that should be borne in mind when addressing the issue of pensions and flex are:

- **Pension modeller**

Raising the profile of pensions through flex will often make employees think about their pension provision more frequently. It also requires them to think about pensions in conjunction with all their other benefits, and their remuneration in general, and not in isolation. The inclusion of a pension modelling facility within the flexible benefits communication module can help employees with their decision-making process.

- **Communication**

If pensions are included in a flexible benefits scheme, communication becomes a very important issue. If employees are making decisions on their pension provision they should have all the necessary information available to help them make such decisions in an informed manner. There is no point requiring decisions to be made at a particular point in the year, then having pension benefit statements provided after the decisions have been taken. The timing of distribution of information is critical.

- **Contractual obligations**

Many employment contracts make reference to the pension schemes the employer provides for its employees. It is important when looking at incorporating a pension scheme into a flex plan to see what your contractual obligations are, to establish whether there are any obstacles to the approach you intend to adopt.

Table 5 | Case studies: pension provision

Companies	Initial pension provision	Further pension provision	Additional future pension provision
B	none	Pension top-up	Flexible pensions
C	AVCs	none	none
D	Defined benefits	Defined contribution	none
F	Group personal pension	none	none

- **Pension scheme rules**

The trust deed and rules of most pension schemes are very specific on what the benefits of the scheme are and how the scheme works. Introducing flexibility into the pension scheme may or may not be possible and will nearly always require changes to the scheme rules and trustee approval for the changes. It is therefore important that these issues should be explored very early on in the process, so that you are aware of exactly what can and cannot be achieved.

- **Salary sacrifice**

Salary sacrifice arrangements for pension schemes are a way of saving National Insurance contributions on the employee contributions. This is achieved by reclassifying employee contributions as voluntary reductions in earnings in return for an employer contribution into the pension scheme (with no obligation on the employer to make the contribution). The savings generated are often used to cover the costs of the flex scheme implementation.

There is nothing wrong with such an approach, and in fact using a flex plan for the vehicle rather than adopting this approach in isolation is much easier. You do, however, need to make sure that you consider all the issues and knock-on effects, for example:

- Reduced NIC leads to reduced state benefits.

- Reduced earnings will affect earnings-related benefits, eg life insurance and PHI.

- Reduced earnings will affect the maximum amounts that can be paid into the pension scheme.

- For group personal pension plans and stakeholder arrangements the different way the tax relief works for employer and employee contributions will affect the amounts being paid into the pension scheme and the employee's own tax liability.

Future legislation on age, retirement and pensions

Organisations considering introducing a flexible benefits scheme should consider the likely impact of such government proposals as: a single lifetime limit on how much someone can save in a pension; a limit on the amount of money an individual can put into a pension scheme in any given year; allowing people to receive an occupational pension from their current employer.

This chapter covers:

- tax and National Insurance issues

- legal issues

- equal opportunities and discrimination

- business transfers.

5 | Tax and employment law issues

Introduction

It is important that any organisation that is introducing a flexible benefits scheme understands the impact of the scheme's taxation treatment and the possible consequences of not dealing with any employment law issues that may arise.

The correct tax treatment will ensure that the benefits delivered to employees are maximised and the cost of the scheme to the employer is minimised.

The employment law issues may not always be immediately apparent, and can be a trap for the unwary.

Tax and National Insurance issues
Employee's position

As a flexible benefit scheme consists of a salary element, a benefit-in-kind element taxed under specific rules and a voluntary element purchased by the employee, it is important for employees to be aware of the tax impact of their choices on their net pay.

Also, if employees are members of a final salary pension scheme, then if they choose to trade their taxable benefit (eg salary) for a non-taxable benefit (eg medical screening), then this could affect the way in which an employee's pension benefits are calculated.

> 'The correct tax treatment will ensure that the benefits delivered to employees are maximised and the cost of the scheme to the employer is minimised.'

Employer's position

The employer will be seeking to ensure that any costs incurred in implementing the flexible benefits scheme are allowable as a deductible expense in determining taxable profits, because the costs have been incurred in rewarding employees.

Legal issues
Changing the terms of an employee's contract

It is likely that the introduction of a flexible benefit scheme will result in changes to an employee's contract of employment with his or her employer, so it is important at the outset that employers consider how this will be achieved.

Changes to an existing contract of employment can normally only be effected by:

- Mutual consent – the employer and employee agree to the changes to the existing contract.

- Implied consent – for example, an employee continuing to work for an employer after the change has taken place and while the employee is aware of the change.

- Contractual authority – sometimes contracts of employment expressly reserve a right for the employer to alter the terms of the contract. An employer should not rely upon such clauses as courts very often give them only a limited interpretation.

- Collective agreements – variations to contracts of employment can arise under the terms of a collective agreement, usually between the employer and a trade union. Such collective agreements are normally expressly incorporated into an employment contract. An employee must be informed if collective agreements are in place and whether they apply to their contract. This is part of the information an employer must provide to an employee after they have commenced employment. If the collective agreements have been incorporated and changes are made, then the employee's terms will be altered irrespective of whether the employee is a member of the union.

- Unilateral variation – if the employer decides to proceed with a change to an employee's contract of employment without obtaining consent, then this will amount to a breach of contract by the employer. If it is a fundamental change, the employee may be entitled to resign and claim constructive dismissal. Whether the employee resigns or not he/she may still be able to bring a claim for breach of contract in either the civil courts or before an employment tribunal. Employers should not proceed in this way as it may give rise to costly claims.

- Termination with notice and the offer of a new contract – another possibility for employers is to terminate an employee's contract with notice, thereby avoiding any breach of contract claim, and then offer the same employee a new contract with the new terms. However, the risk in proceeding in this way is that because there has been a termination, then it may give rise to an unfair dismissal claim. However, in most instances, it will be unlikely that the introduction of a flexible benefits scheme on its own would result in the employer having to terminate employees' contracts with notice and offer them all new terms and conditions.

Equal opportunities and discrimination

It is important that at the design and planning stage of any flexible benefits scheme, some thought is given to ensure that it offers equal access and opportunities to all employees. This will enable an employer also to consider whether the introduction of the flexible benefits scheme will give rise to discrimination claims.

This is likely to arise in the context of discrimination on the grounds of:

- sex

- race

- disability

- sexual orientation (from December 2003)

- religion or belief (from December 2003)

- age (from October 2006).

There are certain limited circumstances in all of these areas when it may be possible for an employer to treat people differently as a result of their sex, race, etc. However, in the context of a flexible benefits package it is difficult to see any of the exceptions applying.

An employer must also ensure that the terms of any flexible benefits scheme do not result in any less favourable treatment towards:

- part-time workers or

- fixed-term contract workers.

Business transfers

Employers sometimes look to introduce a flexible benefits scheme as a way of harmonising different sets of employee benefits following a business transfer.

However, in these circumstances, the Transfer of Undertakings (Protection of Employment) regulations (TUPE) may apply. On such a transfer, the employees of the organisation taken over automatically become the employees of the new organisation on the terms and conditions they enjoyed previously.

Employees cannot waive the benefit of TUPE. If any variation of employees' contracts is to be carried out after the transfer of an undertaking, then it will be necessary to consider TUPE very carefully, because, if the sole reason for the variation is the transfer, then the variation is likely to be ineffective.

This is an extremely complex area and will require careful consideration if the intention is to introduce a flexible benefits scheme following a business transfer.

This chapter covers:

◘ developing an integrated communication strategy

◘ the role of technology in the strategy and

◘ the various types of documentation typically associated with a flex plan.

6 | Documentation, scheme launch and communications

Introduction

Today, communication is often about managing expectations and perceptions. A flexible benefits scheme should be uniquely branded, based on internal marketing. Many organisations have therefore given a name to their flexible benefits scheme.

Education is the vital component of communicating a flexible benefits scheme. Employees should understand the options available to them and the consequences of their decisions, because they will ultimately be responsible for them. As communications is such a complex and vital part of the successful introduction of a flexible benefits scheme, employers may consider creating a launch project team to manage this part of the process. A good communication strategy sets out to answer the following questions:

- How is a unique brand and style best designed?
- What needs communicating?
- Who are you communicating to?
- What media do you need to use?
- Who will be the communicator?
- What is the best timing?
- How are communication difficulties overcome?

Communication stakeholders

Flexible benefits schemes are dependent on partnership between all the stakeholders. Therefore, the first task is to identify the various communication stakeholders; these can include the following:

- employees
- system and product suppliers
- senior management
- employee representative bodies
- line managers.

Developing an integrated communications strategy

The next stage is to develop a strategy that recognises the difference between informal and formal communication.

The most powerful form of formal communication is a one-to-one meeting. In reality, there is not enough time to do this for every employee and the process would be costly. However, the closer you can mimic this 'one-to-one' philosophy, the more effective the communications strategy will be. Consideration should also be given at this time to how the scheme will be communicated with line managers, because they will probably be fielding questions from their teams on what is being introduced and why, and how it will work in practice.

There are five main parts of the communications strategy:

1. Announcement

The usual strategy adopted is to begin the process by sending out a letter to individuals, informing them that the company is considering a new employee benefits initiative. As with advertising, this notice does not contain any answers, but merely states the intent of the organisation to do something.

2. Launch

The launch itself should be tailored to the unique culture of the organisation. The organisation must make sure that its launch encourages people to attend and also to listen. It is important for employees to clearly understand what their options are, and the consequences of certain choices. There should be an opportunity for employees to ask any questions they have, either at the launch event or later, via email or letter.

Q: Did your employees have problems understanding the scheme?

A: No, but interest needs to be kept up with stakeholders all the time; for instance, we are now starting communication workshops for next year. We believe that in addition to the launch, you have to keep relaunching the scheme every year or interest tails off. Some employees found it confusing that they had to renew their choices this year as they thought it just carried on; so you need to make that clear to staff at the start. We have steered clear of including pensions within the scheme as we felt it was too contentious.
Company A

3. Surgeries and helplines

Usually as a result of the presentation, the majority of employees will have a clear understanding of what is on offer, the process and how to go about making their choices. However, there may be some people who still need further help. Running a series of surgeries and/or helplines can provide this. The amount of time and resources available usually dictates the level of this support.

4. Communication catalysts

The success of the above process is very much dependent on the company's choice of individuals to run it. When choosing the communication catalysts, the key points to consider are:

- Who are the most able people within the organisation to explain and sell the scheme?

- What arguments can we give them to sell the scheme and what information can we give them to explain how it works in an easy and understandable manner?

- Ensure a contingency plan is in place to cater for any comments that staff may have.

5. Feedback and modification

The last part of developing an integrated communication strategy is to develop systems and procedures that allow close monitoring of the current situation. The organisation should not be afraid to correct its communication strategy and modify it in response to the information obtained.

The use of technology

Technology is there to assist and enhance the flexible benefits scheme, not to dictate it. Companies should not jump just for the sake of it. Technology is topical and grabs the headlines, but is no good without a focused and well-thought-through strategy supporting it. Before deciding how to use technology to communicate, it is first necessary to consider and decide 'who', 'what', 'where' and 'when'. Answers to these will steer the organisation towards the correct 'how'. Key points to consider are:

- Who is the target audience?

- What is going to be communicated?

- Where and when is it best to introduce technology?

- What is the best way to introduce technology?

- What will the security issues be?

Flexible Benefits
Documentation, scheme launch and communications

> *'To a large degree, the success or failure of a flexible benefits scheme can hinge on the quality of the organisation's communications.'*

Documentation

To a large degree, the success or failure of a flexible benefits scheme can hinge on the quality of the organisation's communications. Scheme documentation is an integral part of these communications and, by getting the documentation right, a company will go a long way towards successfully promoting the scheme and ensuring its effective installation. It is important that employers adopt a communications style that staff find easy and accessible.

The most important issue, though, is that employees clearly understand what options are available and the consequences of the choices they make, and accept responsibility for them. This means that education is more important than promotion and the role of documentation in delivering this objective.

There are five main types of document required for a flexible benefits scheme:

1. Announcements

The new scheme strategy needs to involve some form of announcement covering the decision to introduce a new flexible benefits scheme, an outline of how the scheme will work, and details of opportunities for employees to obtain further information, for example workplace presentations.

Table 6 | Case studies: communications media used

Communications media used for the original launch				
Brochure	Newsletter	Briefing	Leadership teams	Posters and leaflets
Supplier presentations	Workshops	Trade union briefings	Intranet	Email
Memos	Welcome packs	Presentations/roadshows	Videos	Payslips
Media used in addition now				
PEPs	Invitation letter	Line manager briefing packs	Training sessions	Targeted focus groups
Employee 'self-service'	Workflow messages	Benefit statements	Staff questionnaire	
Most successful media				
Brochure	Newsletter	Suppliers visits	Line manager briefing packs	Training sessions
Focus groups	Presentations/roadshows	Email	Benefit statements	Intranet

2. Employee handbook

The scheme guide or handbook has to provide full details of a potentially quite complex arrangement, and it has to do this in a manner that will enable employees to fully understand and appreciate the flexible benefits scheme. Employers with very distinct workgroups may choose to tailor their message accordingly.

3. Preference form

The preference form summarises the various fixed and flexible benefits that are available, their options and costs. Most preference forms are produced in a format that allows the employee to calculate the mix of their various choices to ensure that they have not exceeded their flexible benefit allowance (as offered in the scheme) or Inland Revenue and legal limits.

4. Benefit statement

Each employee will receive their own personal benefit statement, specifying the benefits they receive at present and the value of those benefits. It is imperative that the employee checks his or her statement and that any errors are corrected.

5. Total reward statements

Many organisations are now moving towards the concept of total reward statements. The technology required to design and install a flexible benefits scheme makes the step towards this relatively easy and enhances both the promotion of the plan and the education of its members. As with benefit statements, total reward statements cover all, or most, of the items that make up a person's remuneration and benefits package.

This chapter covers:

- the management and administration of the scheme

- the various reporting systems that will probably need to be established.

7 | Management and administration

Management

In the past, complexity and cost of administration have been major barriers to introducing flexible benefits. These days, new technology, better ways of working and the availability of specialist third-party administration have helped tackle these problems.

Employers considering flex should be aware from the outset that the management of such schemes involves the co-ordination of several different elements. These elements include:

- administration team
- HR team
- product providers
- helpdesk function
- IT interfaces.

- **Administration team**

The administration team handles the day-to-day running of the scheme. If the employer is administering the scheme in-house, then the administration team will probably be part of the HR function. But if it is outsourced, then the administrative team will be the third-party provider.

Sound, robust administration processes, with clear guidelines and expectations are needed to make sure processes are uniform across the team. The development of administration guides outlining the processes for new starters, lifestyle changes, leavers and personal detail changes will assist with the management of the scheme.

> *'To deliver a successful flexible benefit scheme to employees there is a need to build a partnership between the HR team and the administration team, especially if the administration team is the third-party supplier.'*

- **HR team**

To deliver a successful flexible benefit scheme to employees there is a need to build a partnership between the HR team and the administration team, especially if the administration team is the third-party supplier.

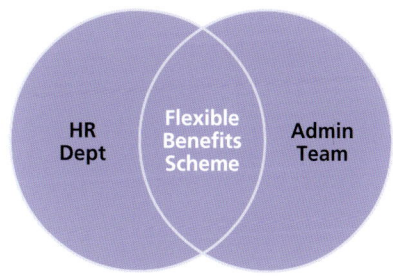

Both teams are reliant on each other and should be working closely together.

- **Product providers**

Good management of product providers reduces the number of issues that can occur within a scheme year. The management of these issues is important and the development of working practices to prevent them from recurring is essential. These issues can include:

- terms and conditions are clearly marketed to staff
- staff understand the options
- clear working procedures are agreed with the administrative team
- payments to providers are made on time.

- **Helpdesk function**

The helpdesk function offers daily support to employees throughout the scheme year. Administrators who have knowledge of the software and scheme design will act as a focal point for employee queries. A tracking system is often used to assist with the management of the calls and allow analysis to take place that will highlight problem areas within the scheme. These can then be used as the basis of future communications with employees.

- **IT interfaces**

The failure of IT interfaces can render a scheme inoperable. Management of this area is very important and service level agreements (SLAs) should be in place to ensure a high level of service is offered to employees. If using a third-party administrator, the same SLAs must be agreed with them.

Q: What made you select a third-party administrator?

A: Initially it was felt that because of the small number of staff covered by the flexible benefits scheme, it could be administered in-house with little effort. However, as the number of staff covered by the scheme has grown, the amount of administration has increased and we have opted for an outsourced online administration process.
Company C

Administration

The administration processes within a flexible benefits scheme are numerous. The following gives a basic overview of the processes carried out by the administration team responsible for the scheme:

- **Enrolment period**

The enrolment period is the busiest period of time in the scheme year. During this fixed period of time employees will be selecting their preferences for the following 12-month period.

- **Post enrolment**

After the enrolment period has closed all the selections made by employees need to be processed, passed to the relevant providers and payroll reports produced. (This is covered in more detail later on in this chapter.)

- **New employee, lifestyle changes, leavers and general employee changes**

New employees within the company may be given the opportunity to join the flexible benefits scheme at an agreed point in time (eg at the end of their probationary period). They should be given a fixed period in which to make their selections (eg 2 weeks, 1 month, etc).

A lifestyle change is an event that allows an employee the opportunity to change their selections partway through the scheme year, eg promotion, birth/adoption of a child, marriage. Lifestyle changes within the scheme will have been agreed during the scheme design stage and rules surrounding product selection will also have been set.

For leavers, the important element in the process is to make certain that providers are notified of the date cover ceased. It is important that the HR function informs the administration team about leavers from the scheme to guarantee correct premiums are paid. General employee changes (eg change of address) should be updated and passed to providers quickly so that they hold correct information on employees.

Reporting

Reporting for a flexible benefits scheme falls into three areas:

1. payroll report

2. provider report

3. management report.

Within each of the above there are two different types of report:

- initial reports at the end of the enrolment period

- monthly reports during the scheme year.

By splitting the reports in this way the volume of data to be managed reduces significantly.

1. Payroll report – end of enrolment

At the end of the enrolment period all employee selections have to be processed via payroll. That includes deductions from salaries and payments back to employees, where they have decided to opt-out of a company-sponsored benefit supplied by the employer. The format and content of the payroll report will have been agreed with the payroll department/bureau during the scheme design stage.

Payroll report – monthly

On a monthly basis new starter and lifestyle changes require processing through payroll.

2. Provider report – end of enrolment period

As with the payroll report, providers need to be supplied with full take-up reports at the end of the initial enrolment period. The format and content of the reports will have been agreed with providers during the scheme design stage.

Provider report – monthly

As with monthly payroll reports, providers should be given changes only for the months following the enrolment period, eg new starters, lifestyle changes, leavers.

3. Management report – end of enrolment

At the end of enrolment a full analysis of the flexible benefits scheme will show the take-up rate per product. This analysis provides valuable information on which products are popular with employees and which are not.

Data can be used to give a visual representation of how the scheme has progressed, as in the two examples shown opposite.

Management report – monthly

The monthly management report is a regular overview of the scheme and incorporates information on new starters, general administrative processes and any issues that occurred during the month.

General reconciliation of scheme

Regular reconciliation between the scheme, payroll and provider reports should take place, eg quarterly. This reconciliation will highlight any errors and appropriate action can then be taken.

Scheme timetable

As the above shows there are a variety of administration tasks that require completion. The development of a detailed timetable for these tasks enables the efficient management of the scheme.

The scheme timetable should be driven by the payroll cut-off date. After the provider reports have been distributed, the whole process starts again and continues until the end of the scheme year. An example timetable is shown in Table 7 on page 44:

Flexible Benefits | **43**
Management and administration

Figure 1 | Critical illness and employee cover

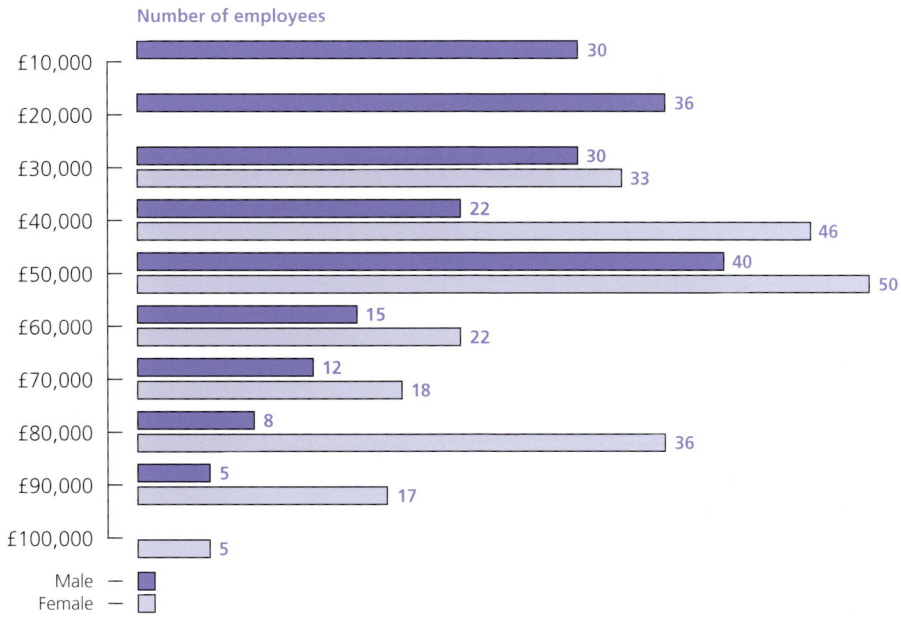

Figure 2 | Travel insurance and cover taken

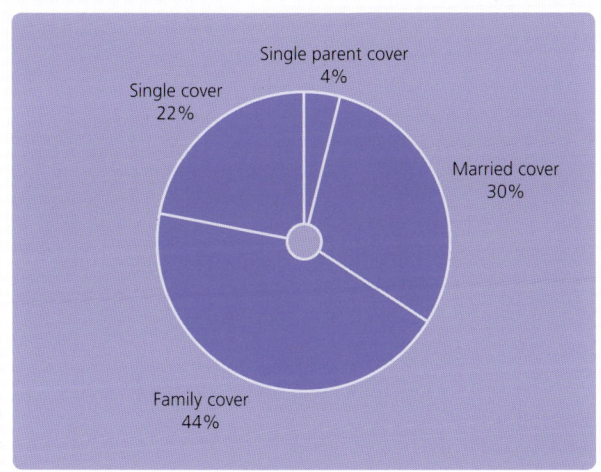

Table 7 | An example timetable

Task	Due date	Responsibility
New starters, lifestyle changes, leavers sent to admin team	21st month	Client HR dept
New starters set-up	22nd month	Flexible benefits admin team
Welcome packs sent to new starters	22nd month	Flexible benefits admin team
New starters make their selections	25th month – 10th following month	Client employees
Changes to deductions	13th–14th month	Flexible benefits admin team
Payroll cut-off	15th month	
Provider reports distributed	16th month	Flexible benefits admin team

This chapter covers:

- the installation and implementation of the scheme and

- the issues concerning the scheme launch and outsourcing.

8 | Installation, implementation and outsourcing

Installation

The final part of setting up a flexible benefit scheme is to install all the various components of the new scheme and to ensure they all work together in 'perfect harmony'.

For this Executive Briefing we have chosen a flexible benefits scheme that is managed online, to demonstrate the issues that need to be considered:

Q: Is the administration easier or more difficult than you expected?

A: It has certainly become more expensive to administer since we first established it. This is due to a rise in the popularity of the scheme and an increase in the range of benefits now being offered. Currently, we are moving towards an 'online' solution and plan to use an outsourced application service provider from next year. This should allow us to cut the administration costs, introduce more complex benefits and improve service delivery significantly.
Company B

Feasibility study for IT systems

The feasibility study will have looked at the IT systems currently in place. Benchmarking against a standard IT specification document will have highlighted any areas for concern, and the study would have identified any investment required prior to the launch of the scheme.

Disaster recovery

A disaster recovery plan needs to be in place prior to any work being carried out on the scheme database. This plan will safeguard any work completed prior to a 'disaster' occurring.

Implementation

The implementation of a flexible benefits scheme follows a very structured approach, and the same approach and project plan can be used regardless of the size of the scheme.

Flexible Benefits
Installation, implementation and outsourcing

Overall project management

The initial project planning stage should take into account all the possible elements involved in the implementation of the scheme. Typical examples of the areas that should be included in the project plan are given below:

- agreement of benefit programme and items to be included, eg pension scheme

- benefit products and providers agreed

- system configuration (functionality, calculations, etc) set-up

- payroll feed (report fed into payroll) agreed and set up

- employee data provided

- security checks (to ensure the scheme cannot be accessed by unauthorised users) made on-site.

- scheme booklets designed and produced

- communication documentation issued to employees explaining scheme

- testing of site (administration and functional)

- site signed off by client

- site signed off by administrative team

- go live – enrolment period.

It is very important to allow enough lead time prior to the go-live date, otherwise any slippage in the plan may prevent the scheme being launched on time.

System set-up

The system set-up is split into the following areas:

- benefit programme

- products

- general system set-up

- employee data.

Benefit programme

The benefit programme for the scheme is made up of the grading structure and associated benefits (ie what benefits are applicable to what grade); the holiday programme and associated rules; the pension scheme and associated rules; and the benefit allowance (ie what amount of money, if any, is being given to employees to spend on benefits).

Products

The set-up of the products within the scheme covers product options and pricing; communication per product (to include details on terms and conditions, application and claims); scheme rules per product (cannot opt out of product, can increase cover, etc); provider rules per product (age limit for dependants, etc).

General system set-up

This area covers the remaining elements that are not included above:

- messaging in the system, eg warning messages

- how the online enrolment form looks and behaves

- reporting, eg what information appears on provider reports per product

- payroll configuration, eg payroll periods, payroll year, payroll report output

- holiday year, eg Jan–Dec or Apr–Mar.

Employee data

It is important that the original data supplied on employees is up-to-date and accurate. This may entail an audit of the data prior to implementing the scheme. Once this is complete the process of maintaining the data throughout the scheme year is relatively straightforward. At this stage, organisations should also be aware that any data collected does not infringe the Data Protection Act.

System testing

System testing is a very important part of a successful implementation.

All elements of the scheme should be tested, and it is a good idea to write specific test scripts covering all possible scenarios. An example of a test script is given below in Table 8.

This clearly shows what you are expecting to happen and what has actually happened. For test scripts that fail, rework will be required to fix

Table 8 | A test script

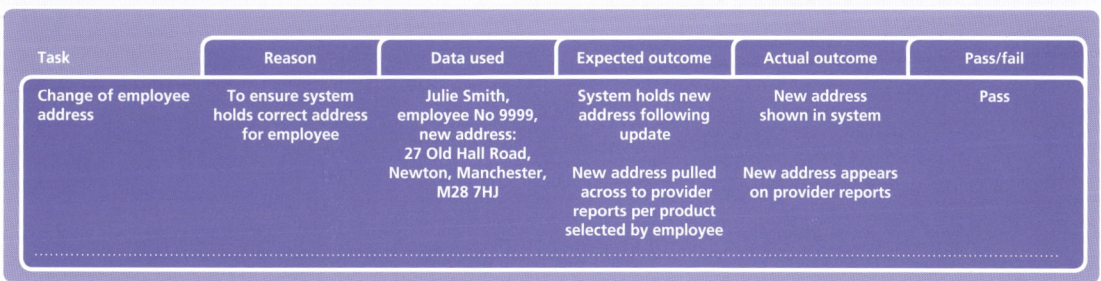

Task	Reason	Data used	Expected outcome	Actual outcome	Pass/fail
Change of employee address	To ensure system holds correct address for employee	Julie Smith, employee No 9999, new address: 27 Old Hall Road, Newton, Manchester, M28 7HJ	System holds new address following update New address pulled across to provider reports per product selected by employee	New address shown in system New address appears on provider reports	Pass

the issue. The same test should be rerun until it successfully passes. Payroll and provider reports should also be carefully tested.

Scheme launch

The launch of the flexible benefits scheme falls into two categories:

- new flexible benefits scheme
- roll-over of existing benefits scheme.

New flexible benefits scheme

The launch of a new flexible benefits scheme should be a high-profile event, with a lot of emphasis on what used to be provided and what is now being offered to employees in terms of their benefits.

The launch may include:

- presentations to employees
- roadshows on new products available, with providers attending
- scheme booklet and other scheme communication
- explanation of new technology being used (if applicable).

Roll-over of existing benefits scheme

As the scheme has already been in place for 12 months or more, the launch of the new scheme year may well be more 'low key' and only focus on new products being provided to employees.

Enrolment period

The enrolment period is the time during which all employees within the company will make their selections for the next 12 months, and is normally the month prior to the start of the benefit year, eg for benefits effective from 1 April, enrolment period is 1 March to 31 March.

During each enrolment period it is inevitable that some employees will not make their selections within the given time period. A decision, during the initial design stage, should be made on how to manage employees who have not made their selections within the set time period, eg default them to core benefits. Another decision is how to deal with those who have not made choices because they are on extended leave, maternity leave or are off work ill.

Post enrolment

After the close of the enrolment period all the selections made by employees have to be processed:

- Correct payroll deductions/refunds have to be given to the payroll department/bureau, prior to the first payroll cut-off date.

- Providers need to be informed of the initial cover selected by the employee (and all the other relevant data they require, eg address, date of birth, dependants, etc). This should be sent to the providers by the end of the first month of cover.

After the above work is complete the scheme settles down into its routine monthly administration, more details of which can be found in Chapter 7 – Management and Administration.

Outsourcing

Outsourcing of any area of expertise is a major consideration for any organisation and is a decision that should be thoroughly researched. Areas to consider when outsourcing the management and administration of a flexible benefit scheme are:

- What are the cost implications of outsourcing? What costs will be charged by the provider per year, per head? Are there any 'hidden costs', eg computer hardware/software that needs upgrading or replacing? Do the benefits of outsourcing the scheme outweigh the cost implications?

- Does the provider have a proven track record? Can you speak to the provider's other clients for feedback?

- Do you want to outsource all areas of the scheme or keep certain areas 'in-house'?

- What are the service level agreements (SLAs) offered by the provider, eg their response time to queries, and are these negotiable?

- What administration procedures does the provider offer? Are these negotiable?

- What disaster recovery plans are in operation?

Table 9 | Case studies: administration systems

Company	Provider	System	Costs £,000s	More expensive than budgeted?	Admin easier than expected?
A	In-house	Online selection	N/A	No	Yes
B	Outsourced	Paper-based	60	Yes	Same
C	Outsourced	Tailored software	17	No	Yes
D	In-house	SAP HR	N/A	No	Same
E	In-house	Tailored software	N/A	N/A	N/A

This chapter covers:

- **The possible developments in flex over the coming years that employers should be aware of if introducing a flexible benefits scheme or reviewing an existing one. For instance, it looks at the possibility of industry-wide flexible benefits plans, or whether more employers will consider allowing staff to use bonus payments to purchase benefits within the scheme.**

9 | Where next for flex?

Introduction

Flexible benefits schemes have now been around in the UK for around two decades. When first introduced, they were seen as very large-scale projects and were really only used by the largest of organisations who had the monetary and physical resources to cope with the implementation and ongoing administration required. With the advances in technology over the past few years, the burden of introducing such schemes has reduced, as have the associated costs. Over the last two or three years, the number of organisations that have taken the plunge and introduced a scheme has grown. There are now estimated to be in the region of 150–250 schemes live in the UK. Some employers within the public and voluntary sectors are now starting to explore the possibility of using flex to attract, retain and motivate staff.

With the growing popularity of flexible benefit plans, there is an increasing desire among the organisations that have had flex for a number of years to develop their schemes to make them more appealing to employees and to bring further advantages for the employer. This desire, combined with the increasing expertise of those involved in the field, will lead to more exciting and innovative uses of flexible benefits plans. After all, there is only so far you can go, adding new benefits to the menu on offer, and only so many choices an employee can make!

Q: How do you maintain interest in your flexible benefits scheme?

A: The scheme permeates all people communication whether it is in recruitment literature or in reinforcing messages about the company package. It underlines the business values and contributes to people strategies. Communication is much more co-ordinated and professional. In addition, employees must receive the same delivery of service as given to our members. We are constantly reviewing and adding to our benefits portfolio, ensuring that both the business and employees benefit. It is about innovation, dynamism and evolving the scheme using employee feedback and developments in the environment to maintain its effectiveness.
Company B

Some potential advances in the use of flexible benefits schemes are explained below.

More flexible benefits

Nearly all flexible benefits plans work on the principle that employees select the benefits they want once a year, and cannot change them unless they experience a lifestyle event, until the following year. This works well for traditional benefits that employees do not normally purchase for themselves outside of work, eg life insurance, PHI and private medical insurance.

This is not so convenient though when it comes to the types of benefits companies are now looking to include in flex plans such as PC lease plans, travel insurance, pet insurance and car lease plans. Many employees have already purchased these items themselves and the time when they want to replace or renew them does not often coincide with the flex enrolment period. Employees would like to be able to purchase these benefits at any time – when it most suits them.

Flex plans in the future will no doubt develop into more flexible arrangements whereby employees will be required to make some selections at a fixed point in the year with other benefits being available to be selected continually throughout the year. This will either be achieved through redesigning the administration procedures around existing schemes or setting up voluntary benefits plans that sit alongside the main flex scheme.

Q: Do you have any plans for the future of your scheme?

A: We see the future as choice rather than cost; for employees to have an online dashboard where they can access their own pay and benefit statement, flex details, pension entitlement and company shares.
Company D

Industry-wide flexible benefits plans

Many smaller organisations still feel that the cost of traditional flexible benefits plans is prohibitive, but they do see the value of them and would like to offer them to their employees.

The problem for those involved in the design, set-up and administration of flex plans is that there is still a lot of work to be done in setting up a plan, even for smaller organisations. One of the biggest problems is getting benefit providers for many of the insurance products that form the most popular elements of a flex plan, such as life insurance, private medical insurance and critical illness insurance. For these benefit insurance providers still require full underwriting exercises to be carried out with individual rates applied to each employer. This makes it difficult for flexible benefits specialists to provide generic flex plans, with generic benefit costings.

Insurance companies are waking up to this fact and are realising that they are missing out on the significant smaller to medium-sized (SME) company market. Going forward we are likely to see the emergence of 'off-the-shelf' flex products that smaller organisations will be able to purchase relatively cheaply and slot into their organisations easily.

The development of these schemes will come from a combination of schemes backed by insurance companies, which use fixed rates for the products included, and industry-wide or trade group schemes that will be developed to cover a number of organisations operating in the same fields with similar employee characteristics.

Profit-related flexible benefits schemes

Many flexible benefits plans are currently set up in such a way that the benefits allowance employees receive is directly related to the costs of a range of benefits. Over recent years the cost of many of these benefits, such as private medical insurance and PHI, have rapidly increased, increasing the cost to the sponsoring employer. Often this happens at a time when the employer can ill afford it.

One way of handling this is to create a profit-related flexible benefits scheme where the benefit allowance given to employees by the employer increases in years when profits are good and reduces in years when profits are not so good. Employees can then choose to opt out of some benefits if their benefit allowance is lower or retain the benefits and pay some of the costs from their salary.

These types of scheme are likely to grow in popularity in the coming years as employers look for ways of managing their employment costs.

> *'Going forward we are likely to see the emergence of "off-the-shelf" flex products that smaller organisations will be able to purchase relatively cheaply and slot into their organisations easily.'*

Extended flexible benefits schemes

Most flexible benefits plans are exactly what they say they are – a way of giving employees some choice over how they receive their benefits package.

It is not a giant leap to extend traditional flexible benefits plans to allow employees to have more input over how the other elements of their remuneration package are delivered.

Sharesave Schemes and Share Incentive Plans could easily be added to the menu of 'benefits' on offer, thereby allowing employees to make wider financial decisions in a more holistic way, though this could impact on the administration involved in the scheme.

Annual bonuses could also be incorporated into plans. Employees could then be given options such as:

- taking their bonus as a cash lump sum in the normal way

- having their bonus paid out in monthly instalments along with their basic pay

- putting some or all into their pension plans

- buying additional holiday to put towards a sabbatical.

These types of scheme developments will ultimately prove popular with employees, allowing them much more control over all the financial aspects of their employment.

All in all, flexible benefits plans can, and will, undoubtedly, be used in much more flexible and imaginative ways in the coming years as employees' and employers' familiarity, understanding and competence with such plans improve.

This chapter covers:

- **the main points already highlighted in the book for employers to use as a basis to test how ready they are for flex.**

10 | Are you ready for flex?

What you're doing and why

The key to the successful choice and implementation of a flexible benefits scheme is to establish a clear strategy linked to the overall objectives of the business. There must be a structured framework for its implementation based on clear communication.

> *'The key to the successful choice and implementation of a flexible benefits scheme is to establish a clear strategy linked to the overall objectives of the business.'*

Table 10 | Case studies: goals for implementing flexible benefits

Cultural change	Matching needs of employees with benefits provided	Access to better rates
Maximise electronic communication	Move to single status culture and improve employer brand	Self-service
Reduce tax and NI	Improve recruitment and retention	Reduce the level of administration and the use of paper
Positive feedback from all stakeholders	Better targeting of money spent	Facilitate merger

Table 11 | Case studies: assessing success

Company	Goals achieved?	Take-up	Would you do it again?
A	Yes	13–15%*	Yes
B	Yes	54%	Yes
C	Yes	100% participation	Yes
D	Yes	50+ %	Yes
E	Yes	N/A	Yes
F	Not fully	100% mandatory	Yes

* 100% took up self-service

Project management

- Create a project management team.

- Establish a clear flexible scheme strategy linked to the overall business objectives.

- Ensure a structured framework for implementation.

- Base strategy and implementation on clear communications.

- Deal with infrastructure issues as soon as possible.

- Introduce the initiative at an even pace.

- Establish clearly defined measures of success.

Feasibility study

- Ensure the new scheme will support and enhance the reward strategy.

- Ensure the market-driven issues are clearly understood.

- Identify how flexible benefits can help to address HR issues.

- Concentrate on administration, outsourcing, IT and infrastructure issues.

- Identify, as far as possible, the financial benefits, costs and risks of the scheme.

- Identify what measures you will use in the future to evaluate and monitor the scheme.

Q: How do you measure the success of your scheme?

A: Through staff 'take-up' and feedback from exit interviews and staff satisfaction surveys. All employees participate in the scheme and 95% of staff believe it is a valuable part of their overall reward package.
Company C

Strategy and design

- Base product selection on quantifiable data and not individual desires.

- Ensure robust link between trading salary, bonus and flexible benefits scheme.

- Ensure the administration, IT and internal structure can support the scheme design.

- Ensure whatever strategy is developed that it can be communicated effectively.

Q: How do you rate your overall experience with the other parties involved – payroll, benefit providers, consultants, administrators, etc?

A: Absolutely vital. It currently takes 32 different agencies to contribute to our scheme (18 internal/ 14 external). It just takes one agency to fall short of delivery to jeopardise the whole project.
Company B

Pensions

- Only include pensions in the scheme if there is an existing pension strategy.

- Consider a variety of different pension scheme options.

- Use additional voluntary contributions as option to topping up pensions.

- Also consider using salary sacrifice where applicable.

- Make sure that the design does not contravene any Inland Revenue requirements.

- Consider the input of contractual obligations and scheme rules.

- Consider the impact of future legislation on age, pensions and retirement on the flex scheme.

Tax

- Clearly understand the current tax and National Insurance position.

- For each product selected, define precisely its tax treatment.

- Assess mixing benefits together and the use of salary and bonuses to fund choices.

- Use modelling to ensure the best mix.

- Develop a clear, simple, effective communication strategy, specifically for tax.

Employment law issues

- Consider changes required in terms and conditions to accommodate new scheme.

- Determine how best to change conditions of employment.

- Ensure that indirect discrimination has not been built into the design.

- Consider the possible impact of legislation on employment, age, sex, retirement, etc, on the scheme.

- Ensure any TUPE requirements are carried through into the scheme design.

Documentation

- Plan out how the organisation intends to announce the scheme.

- Use the employee handbook as the main guide for the design of the scheme.

- Design a preference form so that it can be easily changed.

- Ensure pension documentation is changed to suit the scheme.

- Ensure that the message remains far more important than the medium used.

Communication

- Consider establishing a specific launch team.

- Base the communication strategy on a unique design, brand and style.

- Decide what needs communicating, who you're going to communicate to and what media the organisation is going to use.

- Use the most respected communicators.

- Choose timing to ensure scheme is given the best possible hearing.

- Take into consideration all the communications difficulties that might occur.

Q: Is there anything you do not like about flexible benefits?

A: They work well provided employees can see the 'true' value of their overall reward package; we show this figure on their online enrolment form. Pension and flexible benefits often add a significant amount of money to an employee's reward package and it's important this is identified.
Company C

Management and administration

- Decide whether administration of the scheme is to be in-house or outsourced.

- Identify all inputs, calculations, processing and outputs before designing the scheme.

- Ensure all organisational requirements are catered for.

- Ensure administration and management integrates easily with other systems.

- Allow plenty of time to install and test the system.

Outsourcing flexible benefits

- Ensure there are clearly defined reasons for outsourcing.

- Ensure contracts are well-drawn-up.

- Ensure a good, but practical, set of service level agreements.

- Ensure the outsourcer provides a good set of guarantees and performance bonds.

- Make absolutely sure that the contract caters for all eventualities.

Implementation

- Define data requirements as soon as possible, ensuring that records are up to date and correct.

- Install systems as soon as possible to ensure time for commissioning and testing.

- Ensure service standards set are realistic and that they are being adhered to.

- Ensure that all outsourcers are included in the overall planning procedures.

- Make absolutely sure that all the requirements of the Data Protection Act are met.

Costs, savings and risks

- Quantify all potential savings.

- Include indirect as well as direct savings.

- For each element, ensure that all items and eventualities have been costed.

- Use a good model to analyse the risk associated with each element of the scheme.

- A flexible benefits scheme is a long-term project with long-term rewards.

References and bibliography

Ball, S (2003)
'Pressed for flexibility?'. *Employee Benefits*, March. pp 36–38.

Bingham, C (2000)
Flexible benefits. London, Industrial Society.

CIPD (2002)
Pensions and HR's role. London, CIPD.

CIPD (2002)
'Flexible benefits'. *Quick Facts*. December.

CIPD (2003)
Human capital external reporting framework. London, CIPD.

CIPD (2004)
Reward management 2004 report survey. London, CIPD.

Das, S (2003)
The benefits book 2003. London, Employee Benefits.

Employee Benefits (2003)
'Flexible benefits'. September 2003 (supplement).

Hutchinson, P (2003)
Tolley's flexible benefits – A practical guide. London, Butterworth. Tolleys.

IDS Report (2003)
'Lloyds TSB launches new flexible benefits and shares package'. No 886, August. pp 18–20.

Incomes Data Services (2003)
Flexible benefits. London, Incomes Data Services.

Manocha, R (2002)
'Pick 'n' mix'. *People Management*. Vol 8, No 22, 7 November. pp 44–45.

Partington, A (2003)
'Flexing your muscles?' *Payroll Manager's Review*. Vol 17, No 9, July. pp 23–25.

Purcell J, Kinnie N, Hutchinson S, Rayton B and Swart J (2003)
Understanding the people and performance link: Unlocking the black box. London, CIPD.

Saunders. A (2003)
'Keep staff sweet'. *Management Today*. June. pp 70,73,75.

Thompson, P (2002)
Total reward. London, CIPD.

Towers Perrin (2003)
Benefits package for the future: survey results. London, Tower Perrin.

Tulip, S (2003)
'Flexible trend'. *People Management*. Vol 9, No 23, 20 November. pp42–47.

Sources of useful information:

Philip Hutchinson can be contacted at Jardine Lloyd Thompson, Benefit Solutions, 3rd Floor, 55 Spring Gardens, Manchester, M2 2BY. Or by phone: 0161 242 5354 or by email philip_hutchinson@jltgroup.com.

Charles Cotton can be contacted at the CIPD, CIPD House, Camp Road, London, SW19 4UX. Or by phone 020 8263 3277 or by email c.cotton@cipd.co.uk.

For more information of pensions contact:

- **Pensions Management Institute (PMI)** at PMI House, 4/10 Artillery Lane, London, E1 7LS. Or by phone 020 7247 1452 or at www.pensions-pmi.org.uk

- **National Association of Pension Funds (NAPF)** at NIOC House, 4 Victoria Street, London, SW1H 0NE. Or by phone 020 7808 1300 or at www.napf.co.uk

For more information about reward:

CIPD reward forum www.cipd.co.uk/forums
CIPD reward management training
www.cipd.co.uk/training

Equality, Diversity and Discrimination

How to comply with the law, promote best practice and achieve a diverse workforce

Lynda Macdonald

Foreword by Makbool Javaid, DLA

Is unlawful discrimination preventing your organisation from attaining the benefits of diversity and equality? This book provides an insight into all types of unlawful discrimination in Britain, including the new areas of sexual orientation and religion implemented in December 2003. It is designed for busy HR managers, practitioners and for owner/managers of small businesses.

The book:
- focuses on providing practical guidance, ie on what managers should do to ensure they comply with the law
- is written in plain, clear language to ensure that all readers can benefit from it irrespective of whether they have a pre-existing knowledge of either discrimination law or HR
- provides plenty of case examples, checklists, sample policies and model procedures
- includes useful bullet-pointed 'points to note' and action-points lists at the end of each chapter.

Individual chapters examine practical ways of ensuring equality and the avoidance of discrimination in the processes of recruitment, terms, conditions and benefits of employment, employee development and termination of employment. Harassment is also covered comprehensively with a view to assisting readers to work towards a harassment-free workplace in which all workers feel comfortable and able to perform at their best.

visit www.cipd.co.uk/bookstore, or call 020 8263 3387.

Code: CIPD 280 ISBN: 1 84398 048 7

CIPD Law at Work

Legal Essentials

Straightforward answers to your employment law questions

Written with HR professionals in mind

Legal Essentials are subject-specific titles, that offer practical advice on the areas of law that affect you most and at great value for money. They are designed to be read by HR professionals who must have up-to-date knowledge of the law, and include practical checklists, key cases and frequently asked questions, all of which ensure you save time and money.

New Titles in the series

Working Time Regulations
3rd edition

With the Working Time (Amendment) Regulations 2003 now in force, this new edition is particularly timely.
Code: CIPD 239   ISBN: 1 84398 008 8

Employment Tribunals
2nd edition

Covers the entire tribunal process, and offers practical advice on running a case from start to finish.
Code: CIPD 238   ISBN: 1 84398 047 9

Redundancy
3rd edition

Incorporates recent case law, the right to claim redundancy payments and unfair dismissal.
Code: CIPD 232   ISBN: 1 84398 006 1

These are just a few of the titles in the series. For more information visit
www.cipd.co.uk/bookstore, or call **020 8263 3387**.

™ CIPD Law at Work is a trademark of the
Chartered Institute of Personnel and Development

CIPD Law at Work

CIPD Employment Law for People Managers

HR's source of employment law and practice

CIPD Employment Law for People Managers has been specifically designed with you in mind.

This regularly updated comprehensive volume explains employment law in business terms relevant to the way you work.

Here are just five reasons why you can't afford to be without *CIPD Employment Law for People Managers*.

- **Loose-leaf volume** – your one stop resource for employment law.
- **Quarterly updates** – have confidence in up-to-date information.
- **Quarterly Newsletter** – an update of what's on the horizon.
- **Website** – access to the full service at your fingertips.
- **Research Publications** – up to £100 worth of CIPD research reports for free.

Order your no-obligation 28 days' free trial, NOW

Call **020 8263 3387** or visit
www.cipd.co.uk/employmentlawforpeoplemanagers

™ CIPD Law at Work is a trademark of the Chartered Institute of Personnel and Development